TRICK GEOGRAPHY®

WORLD

TEST BOOK

Patty Blackmer

Blackmer Press
Walled Lake, MI

Patty Blackmer holds a Bachelor of Arts degree in English and American Language and Literature and a Master of Arts degree in Secondary School Curriculum with an emphasis in linguistics from Eastern Michigan University. She has taught in both public and private schools. Patty and her husband, Ron, have homeschooled their three sons.

Trick Geography
4425 Newton Rd.
Walled Lake, MI 48390
TrickGeography@outlook.com

Visit our website at:
www.TrickGeography.com

CONTENTS

UNIT 1: AFRICAN TESTS

AFRICAN COUNTRIES

Match the correct country with its number on the page above.

1. _____   21. _____   41. _____

2. _____   22. _____   42. _____

3. _____   23. _____   43. _____

4. _____   24. _____   44. _____

5. _____   25. _____   45. _____

6. _____   26. _____   46. _____

7. _____   27. _____   47. _____

8. _____   28. _____   48. _____

9. _____   29. _____   49. _____

10. _____   30. _____   50. _____

11. _____   31. _____

12. _____   32. _____   **Islands:**

13. _____   33. _____   51. _____

14. _____   34. _____   52. _____

15. _____   35. _____   53. _____

16. _____   36. _____   54. _____

17. _____   37. _____   55. _____

18. _____   38. _____

19. _____   39. _____

20. _____   40. _____

A. Algeria
B. Angola
C. Benin
D. Botswana
E. Burkina Faso
F. Burundi
G. Cameroon
H. Central African Republic
I. Chad
J. Congo Republic
K. Cote d'Ivoire (Ivory Coast)
L. Democratic Republic of the Congo
M. Djibouti
N. Egypt
O. Equatorial Guinea
P. Eritrea
Q. Ethiopia
R. Gabon
S. Gambia
T. Ghana

U. Guinea
V. Guinea Bissau
W. Kenya
X. Lesotho
Y. Liberia
Z. Libya
AA. Madagascar
BB. Malawi
CC. Mali
DD. Mauritania
EE. Morocco
FF. Mozambique
GG. Namibia
HH. Niger
II. Nigeria
JJ. Rwanda
KK. Senegal
LL. Sierra Leone
MM. Somalia
NN. South Africa

OO. South Sudan
PP. Sudan
QQ. Swaziland
RR. Tanzania
SS. Togo
TT. Tunisia
UU. Uganda
VV. Western Sahara
WW. Zambia
XX. Zimbabwe

Islands:

AAA. Cape Verde
BBB. Comoros
CCC. Mauritius
DDD. Sao Tome and Principe
EEE. Seychelles

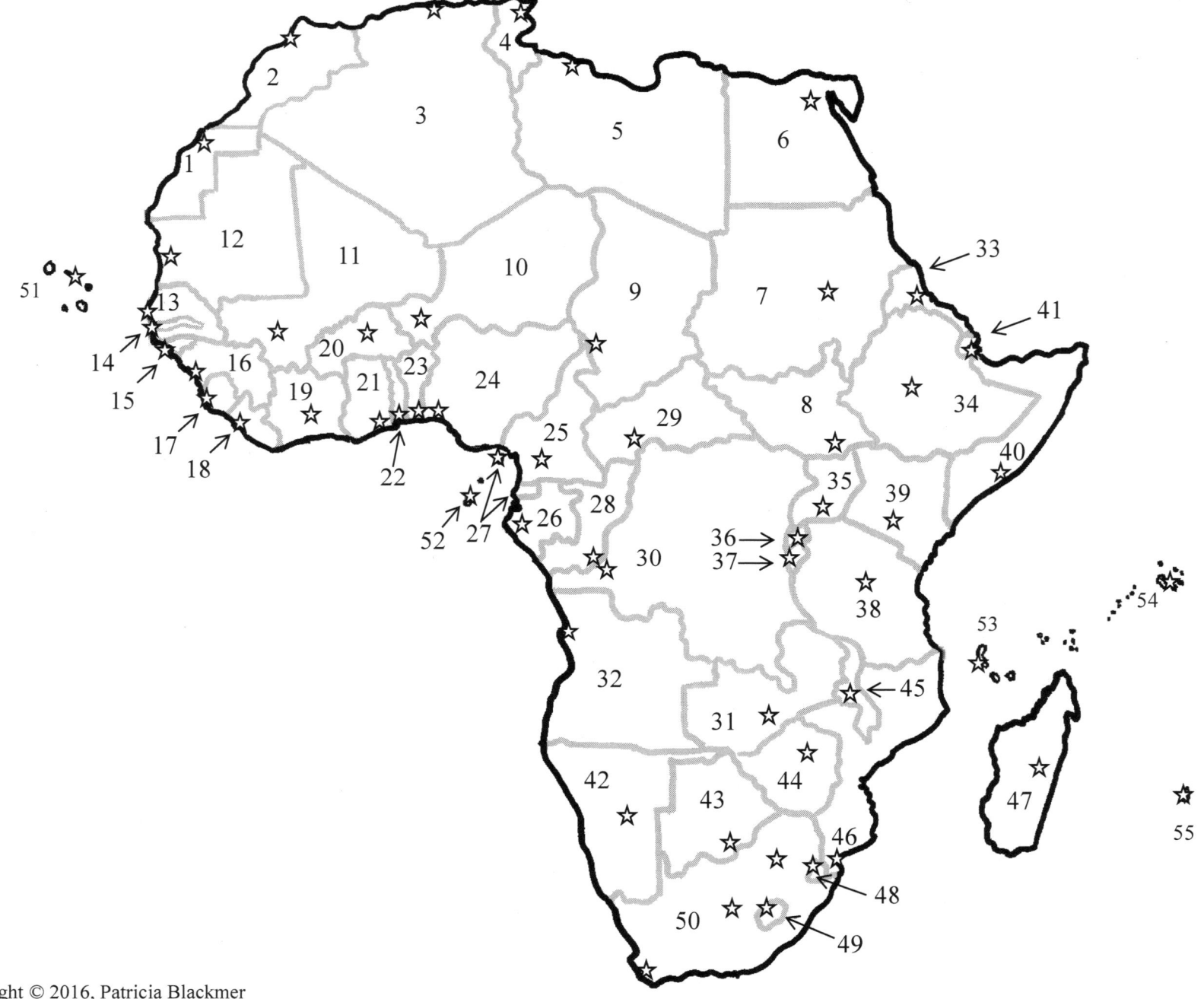

AFRICAN CAPITALS

Match the correct capital with its number on the page above.

1. _____	21. _____	41. _____
2. _____	22. _____	42. _____
3. _____	23. _____	43. _____
4. _____	24. _____	44. _____
5. _____	25. _____	45. _____
6. _____	26. _____	46. _____
7. _____	27. _____	47. _____
8. _____	28. _____	48. _____
9. _____	29. _____	49. _____
10. _____	30. _____	50. _____
11. _____	31. _____	_____
12. _____	32. _____	_____
13. _____	33. _____	
14. _____	34. _____	**Islands:**
15. _____	35. _____	51. _____
16. _____	36. _____	52. _____
17. _____	37. _____	53. _____
18. _____	38. _____	54. _____
19. _____	39. _____	55. _____
20. _____	40. _____	

A.	Abuja	U.	Freetown	OO.	Nairobi
B.	Accra	V.	Gaborone	PP.	Niamey
C.	Addis Ababa	W.	Harare	QQ.	Nouakchott
D.	Algiers	X.	Juba	RR.	Ouagadougou
E.	Antananarivo	Y.	Kampala	SS.	Porto-Novo
F.	Asmara	Z.	Khartoum	TT.	Pretoria
G.	Bamako	AA.	Kigali	UU.	Rabat
H.	Bangui	BB.	Kinshasa	VV.	Tripoli
I.	Banjul	CC.	Libreville	WW.	Tunis
J.	Bissau	DD.	Lilongwe	XX.	Windhoek
K.	Bloemfontein	EE.	Lomé	YY.	Yamoussoukro
L.	Brazzaville	FF.	Luanda	ZZ.	Yaoundé
M.	Bujumbura	GG.	Lusaka		
N.	Cairo	HH.	Malabo	**Islands:**	
O.	Cape Town	II.	Maputo	AAA.	Moroni
P.	Conakry	JJ.	Maseru	BBB.	Praia
Q.	Dakar	KK.	Mbabane	CCC.	Port Louis
R.	Djibouti	LL.	Mogadishu	DDD.	Sao Tome
S.	Dodoma	MM.	Monrovia	EEE.	Victoria
T.	El Aaiún	NN.	N'Djamena		

13

16

4

1

3

6

14

2

5

7

8

8

9

15

Pacific Ocean

Atlantic Ocean

10

12

17

11

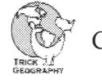
Copyright © 2016, Patricia Blackmer

AFRICAN BODIES OF WATER, MOUNTAINS, DESERTS

Match the correct geographic feature with its number on the page above.

1. _____	A. Atlas
2. _____	B. Blue Nile
3. _____	C. Chad
4. _____	D. Congo
5. _____	E. Ethiopian Highlands
6. _____	F. Kalahari
7. _____	G. Kilimanjaro
8. _____	H. Mozambique
9. _____	I. Niger
10. _____	J. Nile
11. _____	K. Orange
12. _____	L. Sahara
13. _____	M. Senegal
14. _____	N. Ubangi
15. _____	O. Victoria
16. _____	P. White Nile
17. _____	Q. Zambezi

UNIT 2: ASIAN TESTS

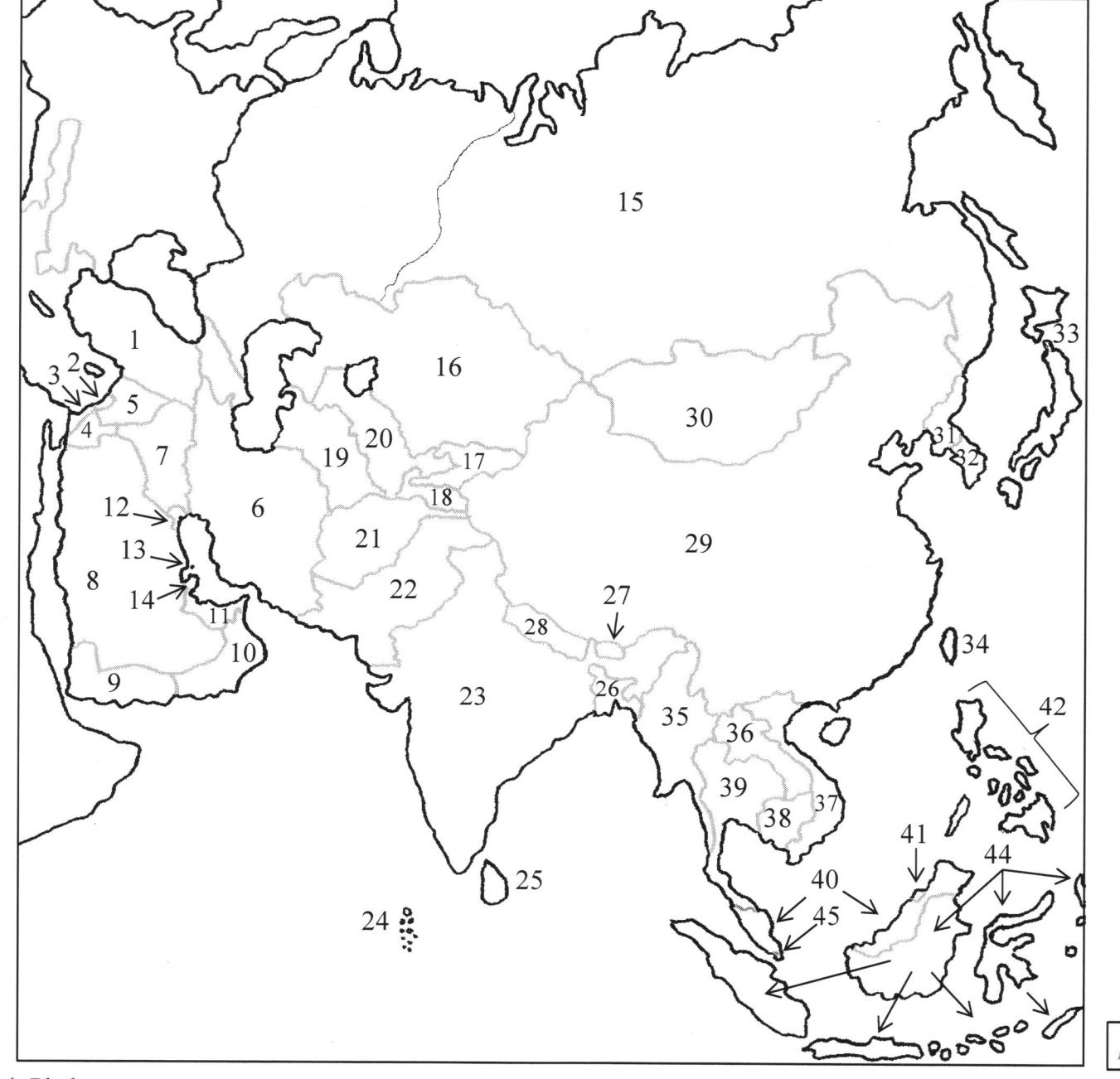

ASIAN COUNTRIES

Match the correct country with its number on the page above.

1. _____	19. _____	37. _____	A.	Afghanistan	S.	Laos	KK.	Taiwan
2. _____	20. _____	38. _____	B.	Bahrain	T.	Lebanon	LL.	Tajikistan
3. _____	21. _____	39. _____	C.	Bangladesh	U.	Malaysia	MM.	Thailand
4. _____	22. _____	40. _____	D.	Bhutan	V.	Maldives	NN.	Turkey
5. _____	23. _____	41. _____	E.	Brunei	W.	Mongolia	OO.	Turkmenistan
6. _____	24. _____	42. _____	F.	Cambodia	X.	Myanmar (Burma)	PP.	United Arab Emirates
7. _____	25. _____	43. _____	G.	China	Y.	Nepal	QQ.	Uzbekistan
8. _____	26. _____	44. _____	H.	East Timor	Z.	North Korea	RR.	Vietnam
9. _____	27. _____	45. _____	I.	India	AA.	Oman	SS.	Yemen
10. _____	28. _____		J.	Indonesia	BB.	Pakistan		
11. _____	29. _____		K.	Iran	CC.	Philippines		
12. _____	30. _____		L.	Iraq	DD.	Qatar		
13. _____	31. _____		M.	Israel	EE.	Russia		
14. _____	32. _____		N.	Japan	FF.	Saudi Arabia		
15. _____	33. _____		O.	Jordan	GG.	Singapore		
16. _____	34. _____		P.	Kazakhstan	HH.	South Korea		
17. _____	35. _____		Q.	Kuwait	II.	Sri Lanka		
18. _____	36. _____		R.	Kyrgyzstan	JJ.	Syria		

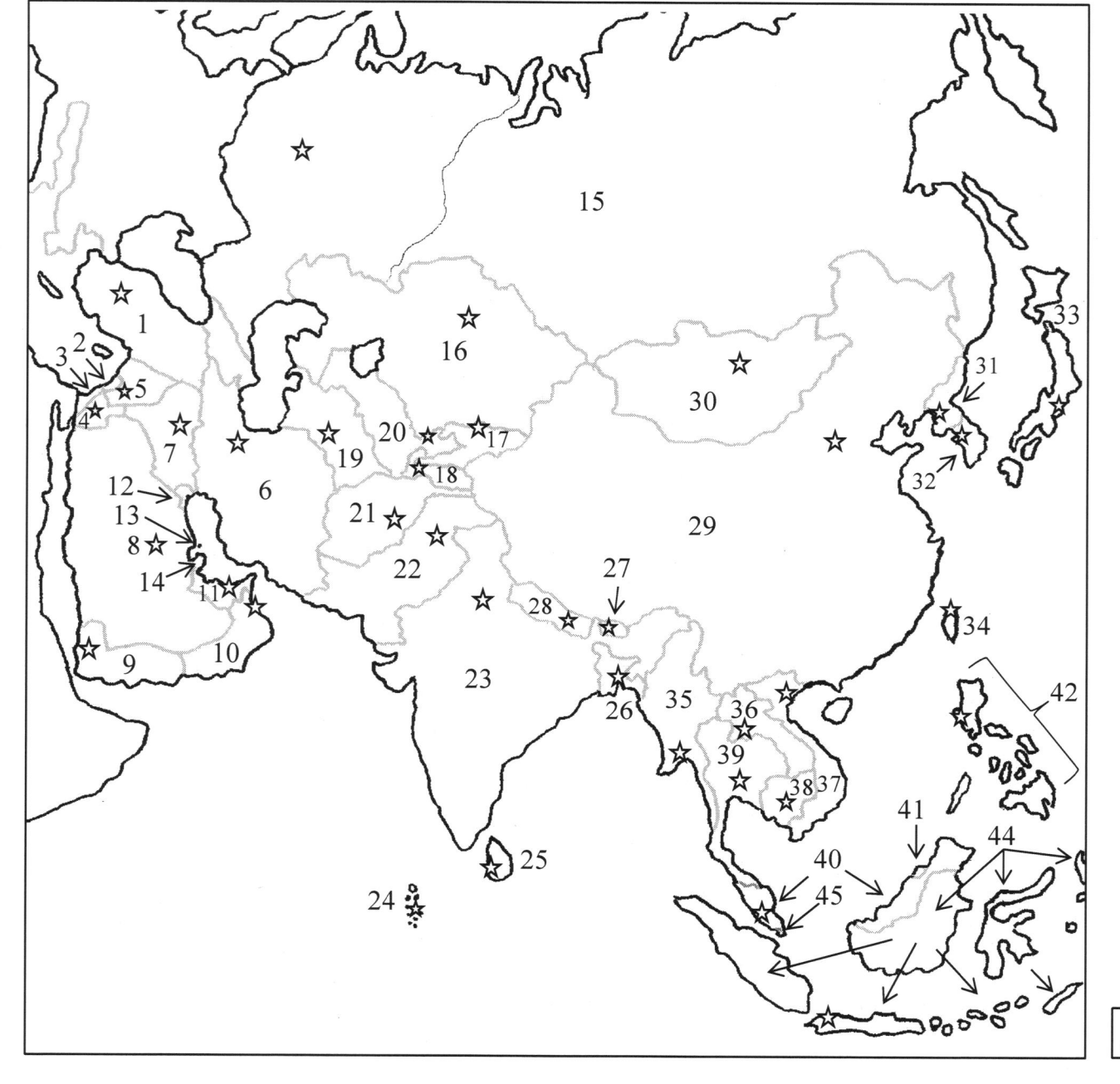

ASIAN CAPITALS

Match the correct capital with its number on the page above.

1. _____	19. _____	37. _____
2. _____	20. _____	38. _____
3. _____	21. _____	39. _____
4. _____	22. _____	40. _____
5. _____	23. _____	41. _____
6. _____	24. _____	42. _____
7. _____	25. _____	43. _____
8. _____	26. _____	44. _____
9. _____	27. _____	45. _____
10. _____	28. _____	
11. _____	29. _____	
12. _____	30. _____	
13. _____	31. _____	
14. _____	32. _____	
15. _____	33. _____	
16. _____	34. _____	
17. _____	35. _____	
18. _____	36. _____	

A. Abu Dhabi	S. Hanoi	KK. Seoul
B. Amman	T. Islamabad	LL. Singapore
C. Ankara	U. Jakarta	MM. Taipei
D. Ashgabat	V. Jerusalem	NN. Tashkent
E. Astana	W. Kabul	OO. Tehran
F. Baghdad	X. Kathmandu	PP. Thimphu
G. Bandar Seri Begawan	Y. Kuala Lumpur	QQ. Tokyo
H. Bangkok	Z. Kuwait	RR. Ulan Bator
I. Beijing	AA. Malé	SS. Vientiane
J. Beirut	BB. Manama	
K. Bishkek	CC. Manila	
L. Colombo	DD. Moscow	
M. Damascus	EE. Muscat	
N. Delhi	FF. Naypyidaw	
O. Dhaka	GG. Phnom Penh	
P. Dili	HH. Pyongyang	
Q. Doha	II. Riyadh	
R. Dushanbe	JJ. Sana'a	

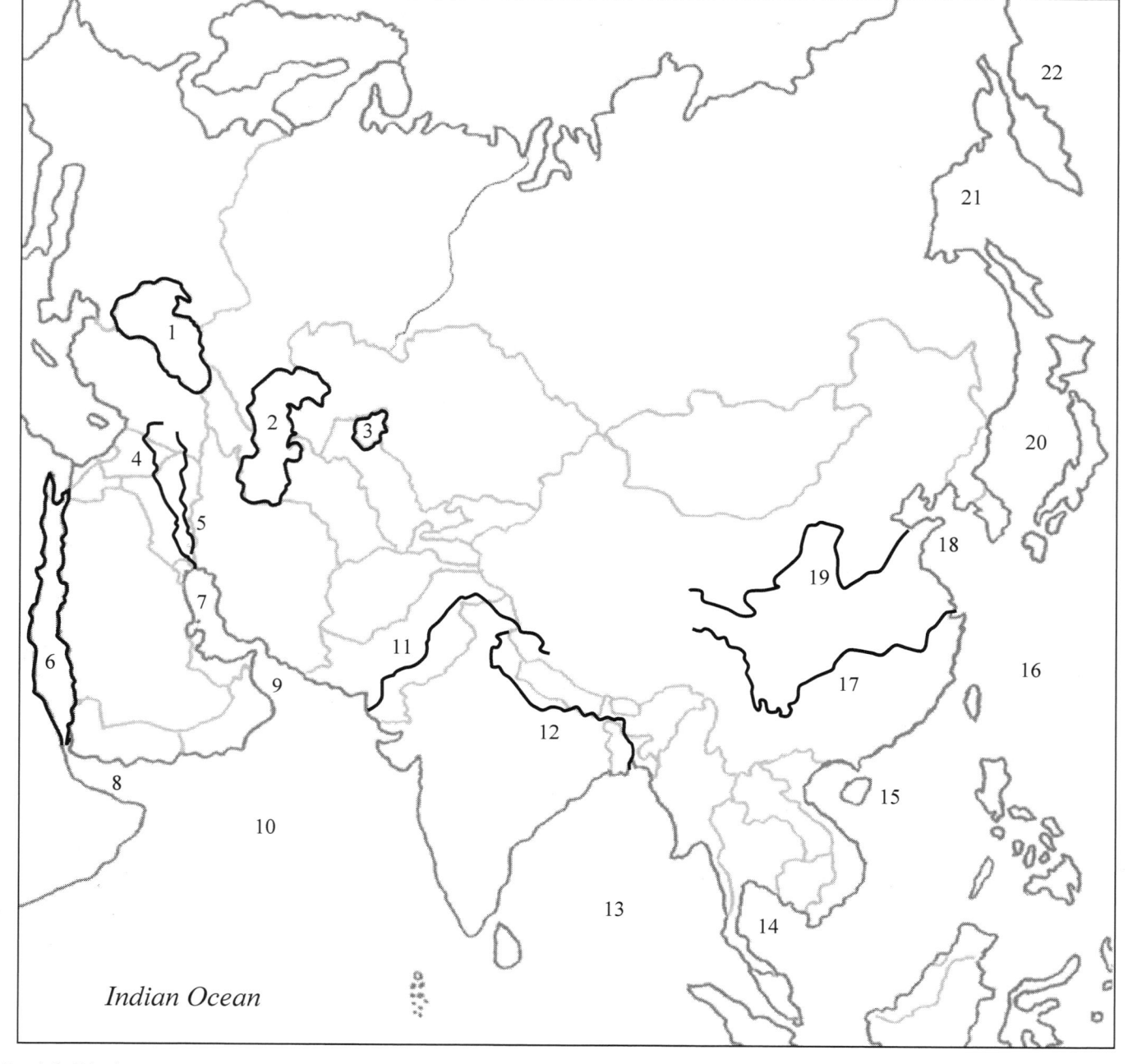

Indian Ocean

ASIAN BODIES OF WATER

Match the correct body of water with its number on the page above.

1. _____	12. _____	
2. _____	13. _____	
3. _____	14. _____	
4. _____	15. _____	
5. _____	16. _____	
6. _____	17. _____	
7. _____	18. _____	
8. _____	19. _____	
9. _____	20. _____	
10. _____	21. _____	
11. _____	22. _____	

A.	Aden	L.	Japan
B.	Arabian	M.	Okhotsk
C.	Aral	N.	Oman
D.	Bengal	O.	Persian
E.	Bering	P.	Red
F.	Black	Q.	South China
G.	Caspian	R.	Thailand
H.	East China	S.	Tigris
I.	Euphrates	T.	Yangtze
J.	Ganges	U.	Yellow River
K.	Indus	V.	Yellow Sea

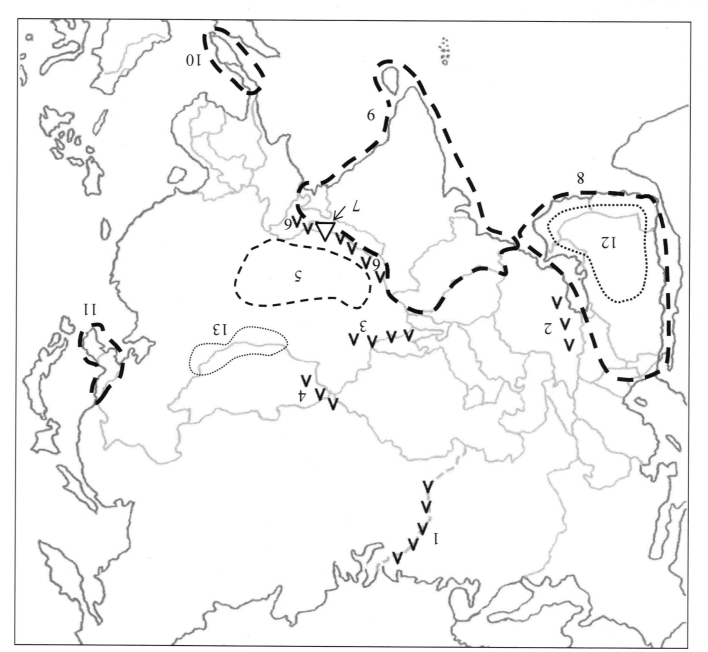

ASIAN MOUNTAINS, PENINSULAS, DESERTS

Match the correct geographical feature with its number on the page above.

1. _____	A. Altai
2. _____	B. Arabian Desert
3. _____	C. Arabian Peninsula
4. _____	D. Everest
5. _____	E. Gobi
6. _____	F. Himalayan
7. _____	G. Indian Subcontinent
8. _____	H. Korean
9. _____	I. Malaysian
10. _____	J. Tibetan
11. _____	K. Tien Shan
12. _____	L. Ural
13. _____	M. Zagros

UNIT 3: EUROPEAN TESTS

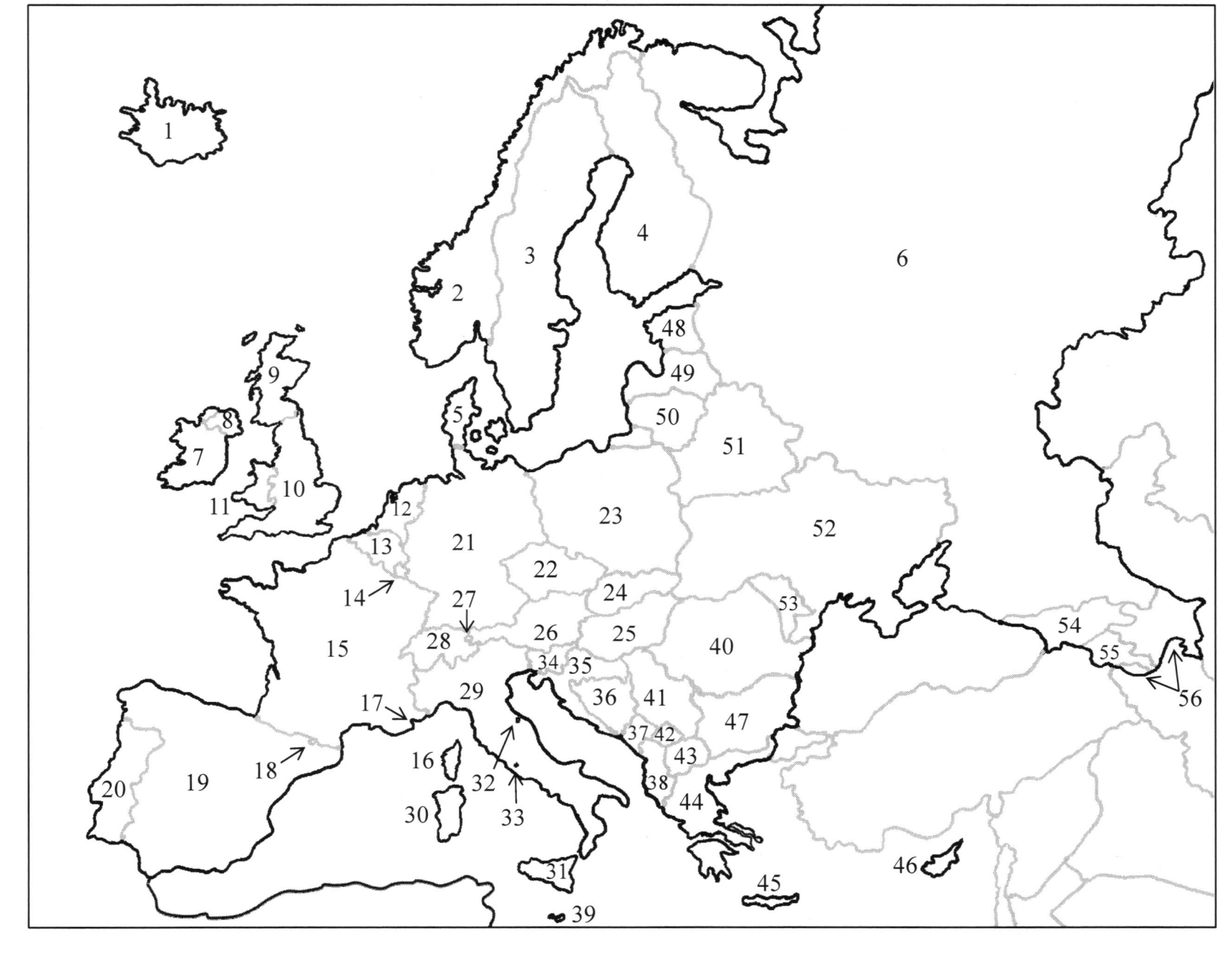

EUROPEAN COUNTRIES, ISLANDS

Match the correct country or island with its number on the page above.

1. _____	21. _____	41. _____	A. Albania	U. Germany	OO. Portugal
2. _____	22. _____	42. _____	B. Andorra	V. Greece	PP. Romania
3. _____	23. _____	43. _____	C. Armenia	W. Hungary	QQ. Russia
4. _____	24. _____	44. _____	D. Austria	X. Iceland	RR. San Marino
5. _____	25. _____	45. _____	E. Azerbaijan	Y. Ireland	SS. Sardinia
6. _____	26. _____	46. _____	F. Belarus	Z. Italy	TT. Scotland
7. _____	27. _____	47. _____	G. Belgium	AA. Kosovo	UU. Serbia
8. _____	28. _____	48. _____	H. Bosnia	BB. Latvia	VV. Sicily
9. _____	29. _____	49. _____	I. Bulgaria	CC. Liechtenstein	WW. Slovakia
10. _____	30. _____	50. _____	J. Corsica	DD. Lithuania	XX. Slovenia
11. _____	31. _____	51. _____	K. Crete	EE. Luxembourg	YY. Spain
12. _____	32. _____	52. _____	L. Croatia	FF. Macedonia	ZZ. Sweden
13. _____	33. _____	53. _____	M. Cyprus	GG. Malta	AAA. Switzerland
14. _____	34. _____	54. _____	N. Czech Republic	HH. Moldova	BBB. Ukraine
15. _____	35. _____	55. _____	O. Denmark	II. Monaco	CCC. Vatican City
16. _____	36. _____	56. _____	P. England	JJ. Montenegro	DDD. Wales
17. _____	37. _____		Q. Estonia	KK. Netherlands	
18. _____	38. _____		R. Finland	LL. Northern Ireland	
19. _____	39. _____		S. France	MM. Norway	
20. _____	40. _____		T. Georgia	NN. Poland	

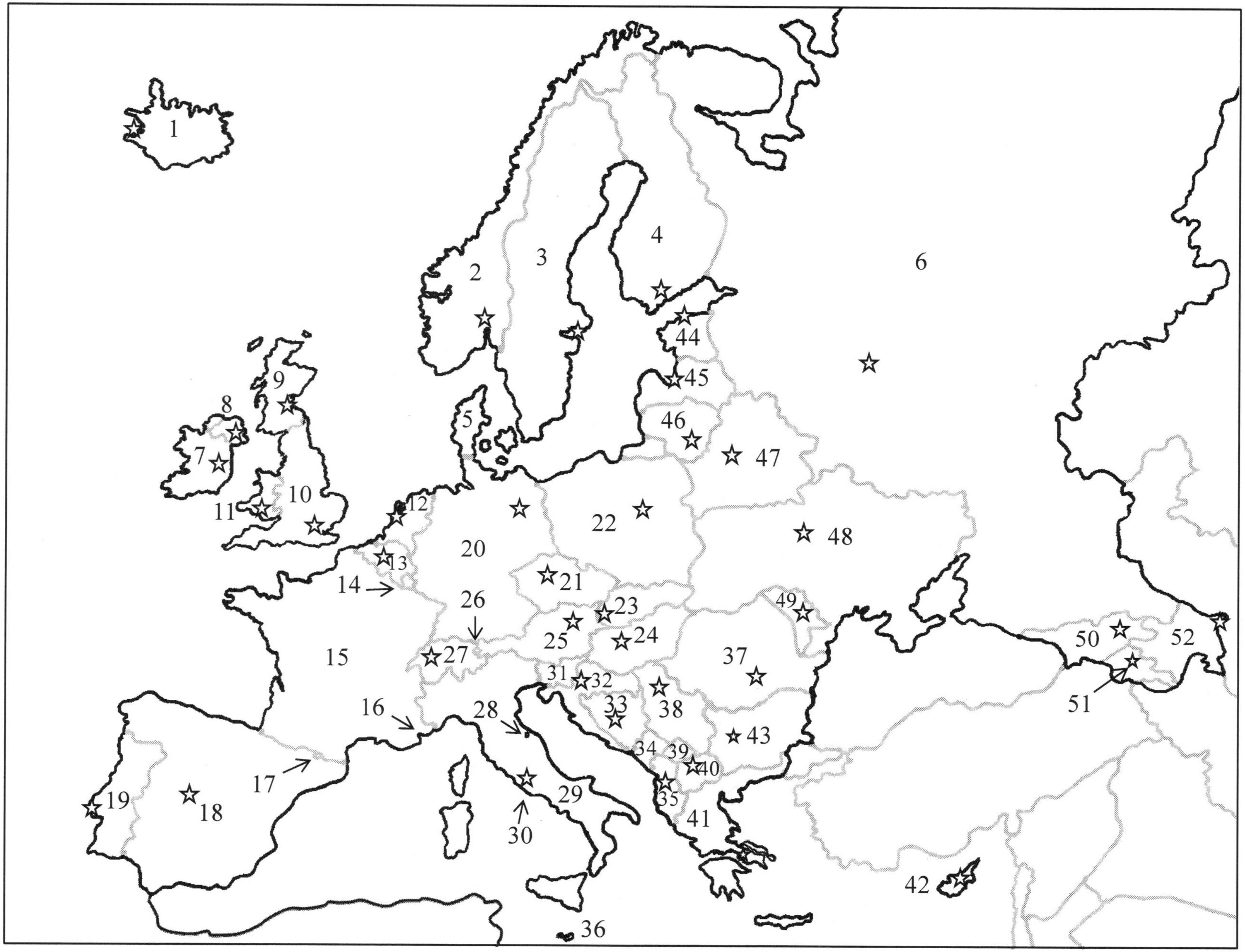

26

1

2   3   4   6

44
45
9
8   46
7   47
11 10 12
13 22
14 20 48
21
26 23
25 24 49
27 37
15 31 32
33 38
16 28 34 39 43 50 52
17 29 35 40 51
18 30 41
19 36 42

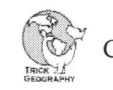
Copyright © 2016, Patricia Blackmer

EUROPEAN CAPITALS

Match the correct capital with its number on the page above.

1. _____	21. _____	41. _____	A. Amsterdam	U. Ljubljana	OO. Stockholm	
2. _____	22. _____	42. _____	B. Andorra la vella	V. London	PP. Tallinn	
3. _____	23. _____	43. _____	C. Athens	W. Luxembourg	QQ. Tbilisi	
4. _____	24. _____	44. _____	D. Baku	X. Madrid	RR. Tirana	
5. _____	25. _____	45. _____	E. Belfast	Y. Minsk	SS. Vaduz	
6. _____	26. _____	46. _____	F. Belgrade	Z. Monaco	TT. Valetta	
7. _____	27. _____	47. _____	G. Berlin	AA. Moscow	UU. Vatican City	
8. _____	28. _____	48. _____	H. Bern	BB. Nicosia	VV. Vienna	
9. _____	29. _____	49. _____	I. Bratislava	CC. Oslo	WW. Vilnius	
10. _____	30. _____	50. _____	J. Brussels	DD. Paris	XX. Warsaw	
11. _____	31. _____	51. _____	K. Bucharest	EE. Podgorica	YY. Yerevan	
12. _____	32. _____		L. Budapest	FF. Prague	ZZ. Zagreb	
13. _____	33. _____		M. Cardiff	GG. Pristina		
14. _____	34. _____		N. Chisinau	HH. Reykjavik		
15. _____	35. _____		O. Copenhagen	II. Riga		
16. _____	36. _____		P. Dublin	JJ. Rome		
17. _____	37. _____		Q. Edinburgh	KK. San Marino		
18. _____	38. _____		R. Helsinki	LL. Sarajevo		
19. _____	39. _____		S. Kiev	MM. Skopje		
20. _____	40. _____		T. Lisbon	NN. Sofia		

TRICK GEOGRAPHY

Atlantic Ocean

EUROPEAN BODIES OF WATER

Match the correct body of water with its number on the page above.

1. _____

2. _____

3. _____

4. _____

5. _____

6. _____

7. _____

8. _____

9. _____

10. _____

11. _____

12. _____

13. _____

14. _____

15. _____

16. _____

A. Adriatic

B. Aegean

C. Baltic

D. Barents

E. Biscay

F. Black

G. Danube

H. Elbe

I. English

J. Loire

K. Mediterranean

L. North

M. Norwegian

N. Rhine

O. Thames

P. Volga

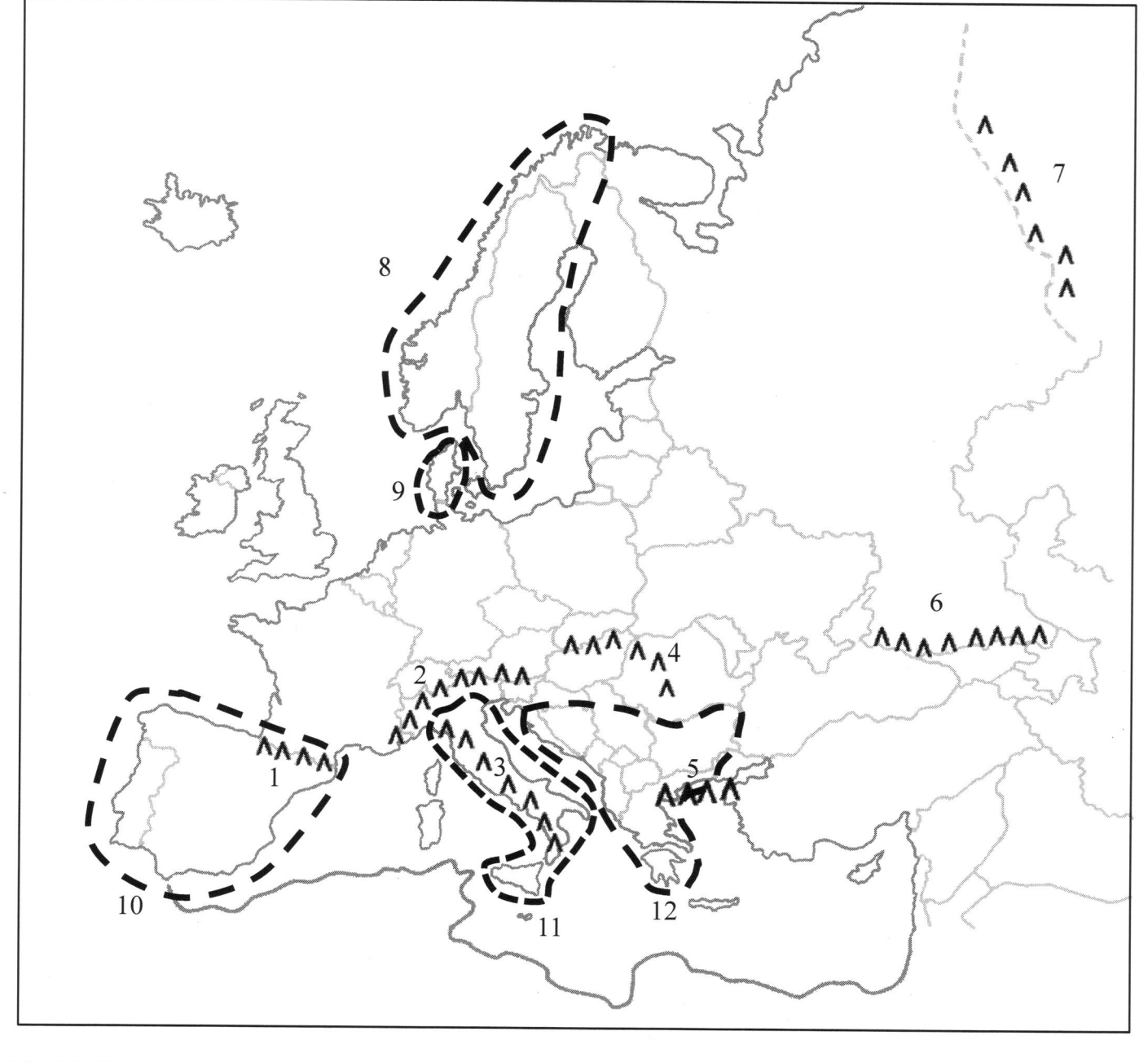

EUROPEAN MOUNTAINS, PENINSULAS

Match the correct geographical feature with its number on the page above.

1. _____   A. Alps

2. _____   B. Apennine

3. _____   C. Balkan (mountains)

4. _____   D. Balkan (peninsula)

5. _____   E. Carpathian

6. _____   F. Caucasus

7. _____   G. Iberian

8. _____   H. Italian

9. _____   I. Jutland

10. _____   J. Pyrenees

11. _____   K. Scandinavian

12. _____   L. Ural

UNIT 4: NORTH AMERICAN TESTS

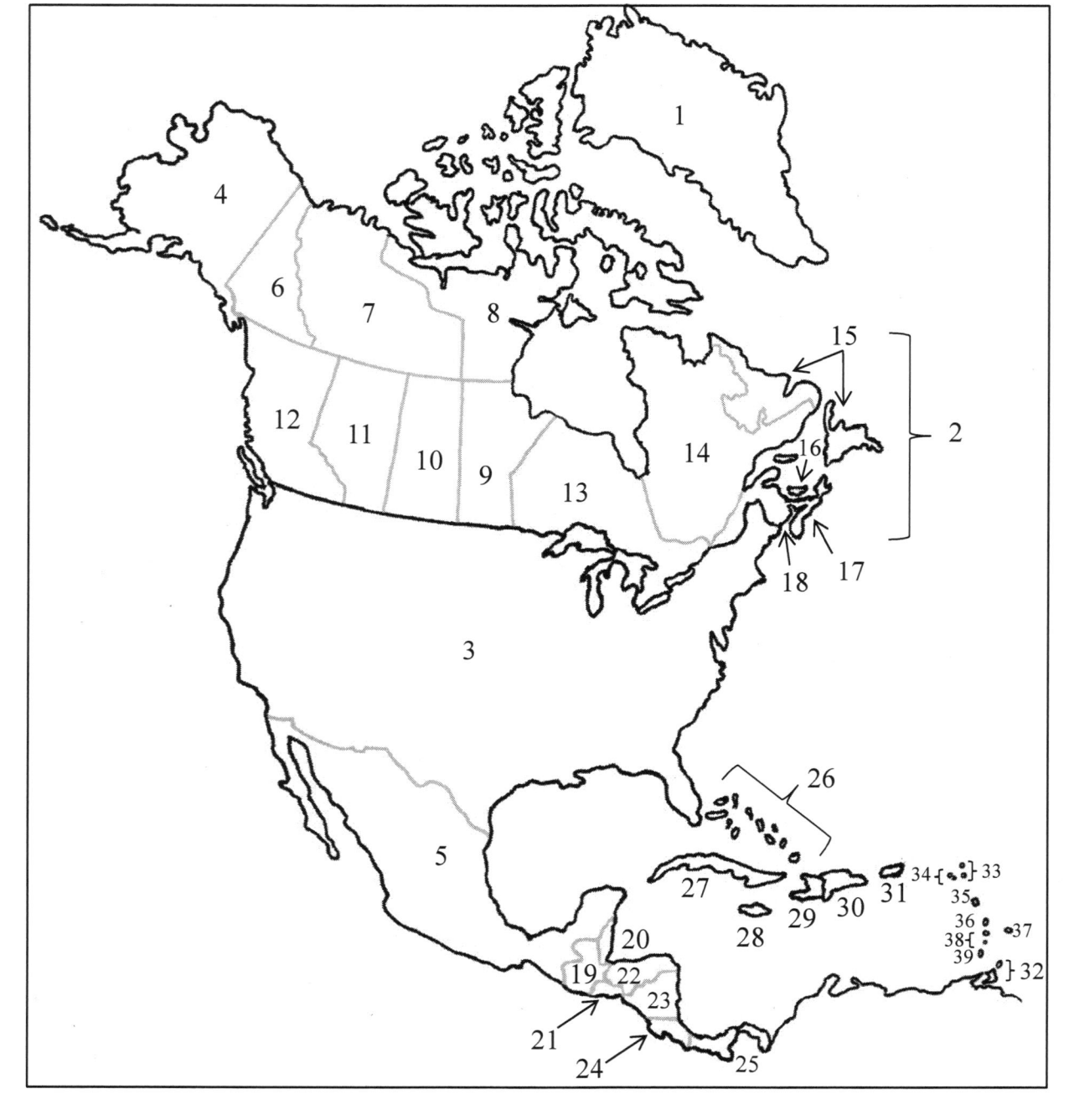

NORTH AMERICAN COUNTRIES, PROVINCES, TERRITORIES

Match the correct country, province, or territory with its number on the page above.

1. _____   21. _____

2. _____   22. _____

3. _____   23. _____

4. _____   24. _____

5. _____   25. _____

6. _____   26. _____

7. _____   27. _____

8. _____   28. _____

9. _____   29. _____

10. _____   30. _____

11. _____   31. _____

12. _____   32. _____

13. _____

14. _____   **Islands:**

15. _____   33. _____

16. _____   34. _____

17. _____   35. _____

18. _____   36. _____

19. _____   37. _____

20. _____   38. _____

          39. _____

A.   Alaska (USA)   U.   Northwest Territories

B.   Alberta   V.   Nova Scotia

C.   Bahamas   W.   Nunavut

D.   Belize   X.   Ontario

E.   British Columbia   Y.   Panama

F.   Canada   Z.   Prince Edward Island

G.   Costa Rica   AA.   Puerto Rico

H.   Cuba   BB.   Quebec

I.   Dominican Republic   CC.   Saskatchewan

J.   El Salvador   DD.   Trinidad and Tobago

K.   Greenland   EE.   United States of America

L.   Guatemala   FF.   Yukon

M.   Haiti

N.   Honduras   **Islands:**

O.   Jamaica   GG.   Antiqua and Barbuda

P.   Manitoba   HH.   Barbados

Q.   Mexico   II.   Dominica

R.   New Brunswick   JJ.   Grenada

S.   Newfoundland and Labrador   KK.   St. Kitts and Nevis

T.   Nicaragua   LL.   St. Lucia

                                       MM.   St. Vincent and Grenadines

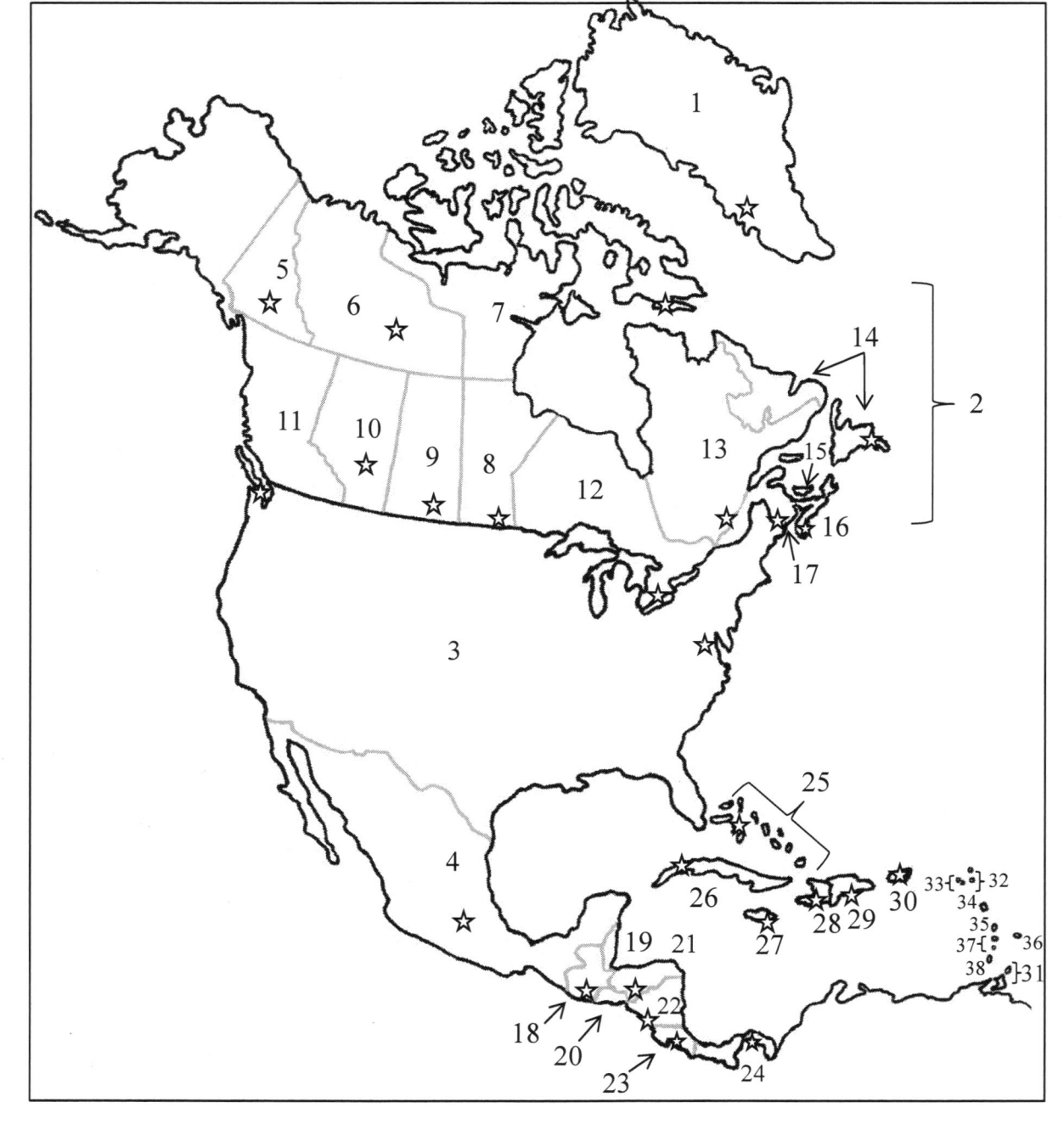

NORTH AMERICAN CAPITALS

Match the correct capital with its number on the page above.

1. _____
2. _____
3. _____
4. _____
5. _____
6. _____
7. _____
8. _____
9. _____
10. _____
11. _____
12. _____
13. _____
14. _____
15. _____
16. _____
17. _____
18. _____
19. _____
20. _____

21. _____
22. _____
23. _____
24. _____
25. _____
26. _____
27. _____
28. _____
29. _____
30. _____
31. _____

Islands:

32. _____
33. _____
34. _____
35. _____
36. _____
37. _____
38. _____

A.	Belmopan
B.	Charlottetown
C.	Edmonton
D.	Fredericton
E.	Guatemala City
F.	Halifax
G.	Havana
H.	Iqaluit
I.	Kingston
J.	Managua
K.	Mexico City
L.	Nassau
M.	Nuuk
N.	Ottawa
O.	Panama City
P.	Port of Spain
Q.	Port-au-Prince
R.	Quebec
S.	Regina
T.	San Jose

U.	San Juan
V.	San Salvador
W.	Santo Domingo
X.	St. John
Y.	Tegucigalpa
Z.	Toronto
AA.	Victoria
BB.	Washington, D.C.
CC.	Whitehorse
DD.	Winnipeg
EE.	Yellow Knife

Islands:

FF.	Basseterre
GG.	Bridgetown
HH.	Castries
II.	Kingstown
JJ.	Roseau
KK.	St. Georges
LL.	St. Johns

 Copyright © 2016, Patricia Blackmer

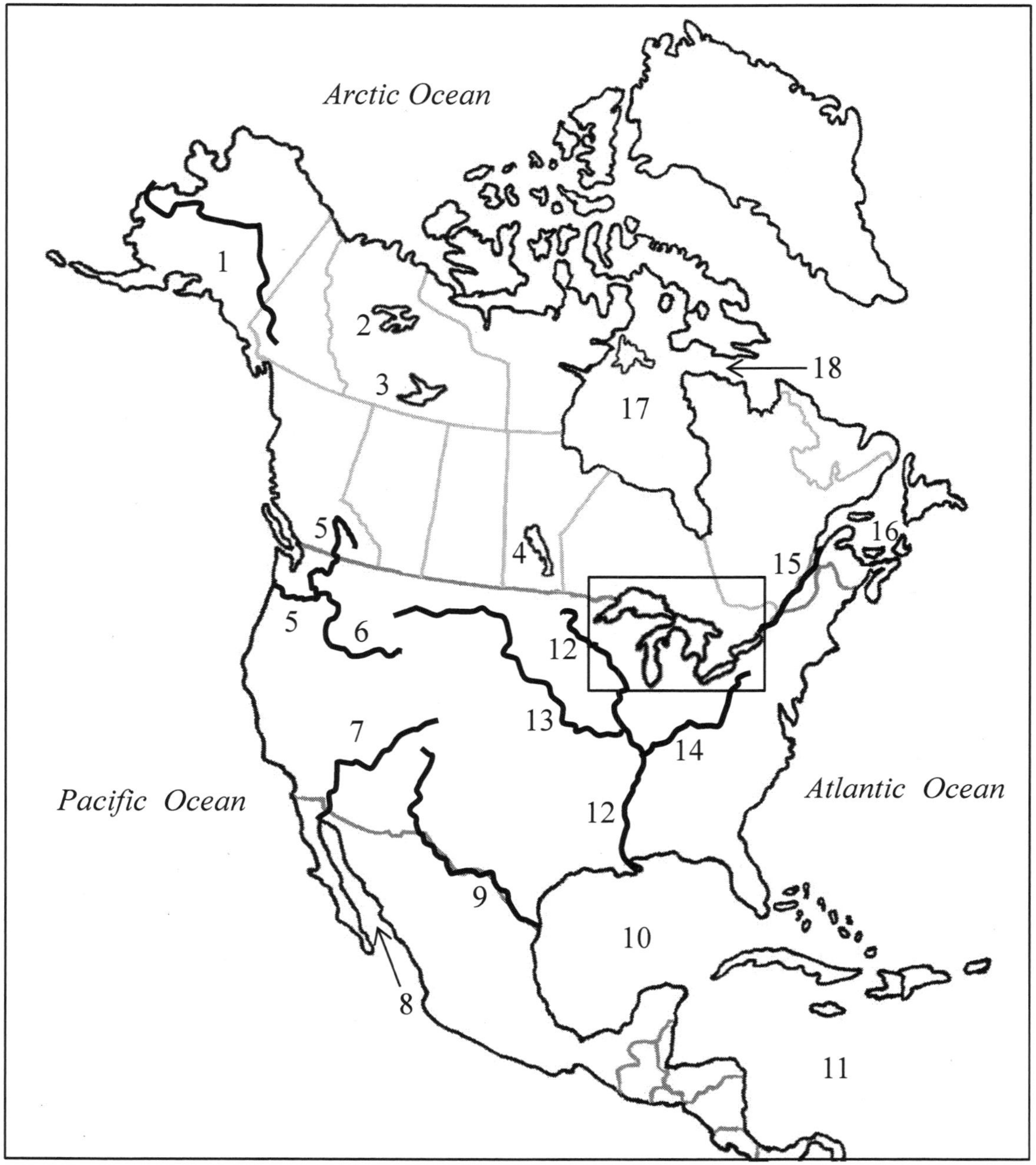

Arctic Ocean

1

2

3

18

17

5

4

16

15

5

6

12

Pacific Ocean

7

13

14

12

Atlantic Ocean

9

8

10

11

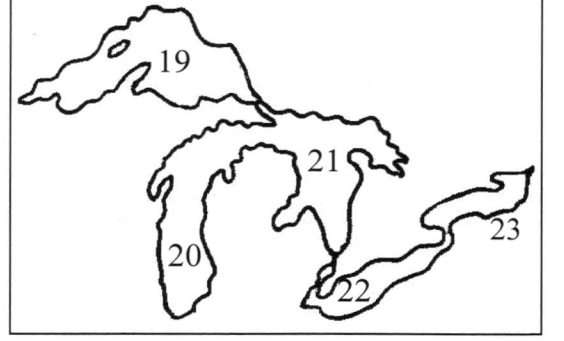

19

21

20

23

22

NORTH AMERICAN BODIES OF WATER

Match the correct body of water with its number on the page above.

1. _____	13. _____	
2. _____	14. _____	
3. _____	15. _____	
4. _____	16. _____	
5. _____	17. _____	
6. _____	18. _____	
7. _____	19. _____	
8. _____	20. _____	
9. _____	21. _____	
10. _____	22. _____	
11. _____	23. _____	
12. _____		

A.	Bear	M.	Missouri
B.	California	N.	Ohio
C.	Colorado	O.	Ontario
D.	Columbia	P.	Rio Grande
E.	Caribbean	Q.	Slave
F.	Erie	R.	Snake
G.	Hudson (bay)	S.	St. Lawrence (gulf)
H.	Hudson (strait)	T.	St. Lawrence (river)
I.	Huron	U.	Superior
J.	Mexico	V.	Winnipeg
K.	Michigan	W.	Yukon
L.	Mississippi		

NORTH AMERICAN MOUNTAINS, DESERTS, PLAINS

Match the correct geographical feature with its number on the page above.

1. _____   A. Appalachian

2. _____   B. Chihuahuan

3. _____   C. Coastal

4. _____   D. Denali (McKinley)

5. _____   E. Great Basin

6. _____   F. Great Plains

7. _____   G. Mitchell

8. _____   H. Mojave

9. _____   I. Rocky

10. _____   J. Sierra Madre

11. _____   K. Sonoran

UNIT 5: OCEANIC TESTS

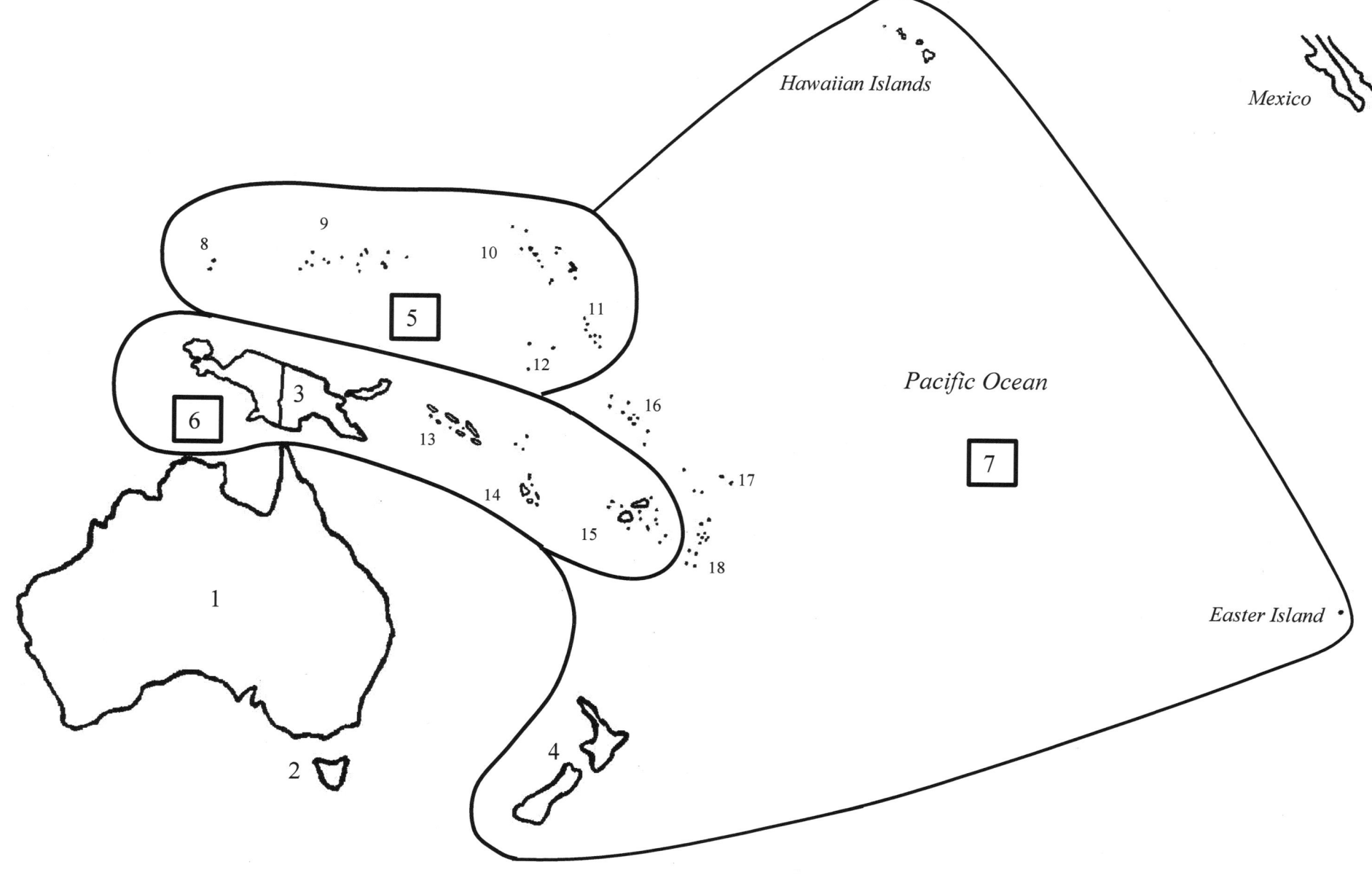

Hawaiian Islands

Mexico

9

8

10

11

5

12

Pacific Ocean

3

16

6

13

7

14

17

15

18

1

2

4

Easter Island

OCEANIC REGIONS, COUNTRIES, ISLANDS

Match the correct region, country, or island with its number on the page above.
(Region numbers appear inside boxes.)

1. _____

2. _____

3. _____

4. _____

5. _____

6. _____

7. _____

Small Islands:

8. _____

9. _____

10. _____

11. _____

12. _____

13. _____

14. _____

15. _____

16. _____

17. _____

18. _____

A.   Australia

B.   Melanesia

C.   Micronesia

D.   New Zealand

E.   Papua New Guinea

F.   Polynesia

G.   Tasmania

Small Islands:

H.   Federated States of Micronesia

I.   Fiji

J.   Kiribati

K.   Marshall Islands

L.   Nauru

M.   Palau

N.   Samoa

O.   Solomon Islands

P.   Tonga

Q.   Tuvalu

R.   Vanuatu

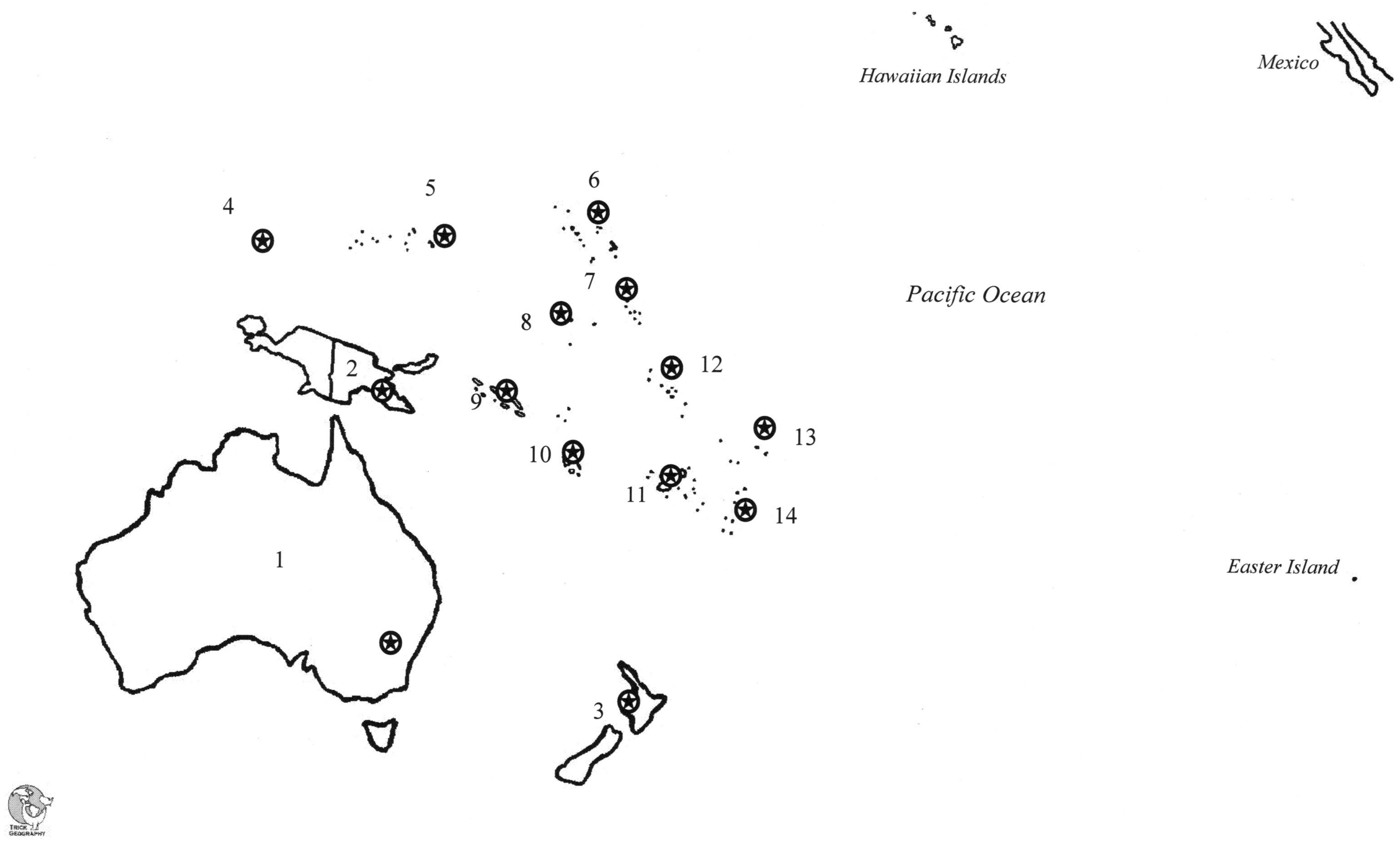

Hawaiian Islands

Mexico

Pacific Ocean

4

5

6

7

8

9

10

11

12

13

14

2

1

3

Easter Island

OCEANIC CAPITALS

Match the correct capital with its number on the page above.

1. _____   A. Canberra

2. _____   B. Port Moresby

3. _____   C. Wellington

Small Islands: **Small Islands:**

4. _____   D. Apia

5. _____   E. Funafuti

6. _____   F. Honiara

7. _____   G. Majuro

8. _____   H. Ngerulmud

9. _____   I. Nukualofa

10. _____   J. Palikir

11. _____   K. Port-Vila

12. _____   L. Suva

13. _____   M. Tarawa

14. _____   N. Yaren

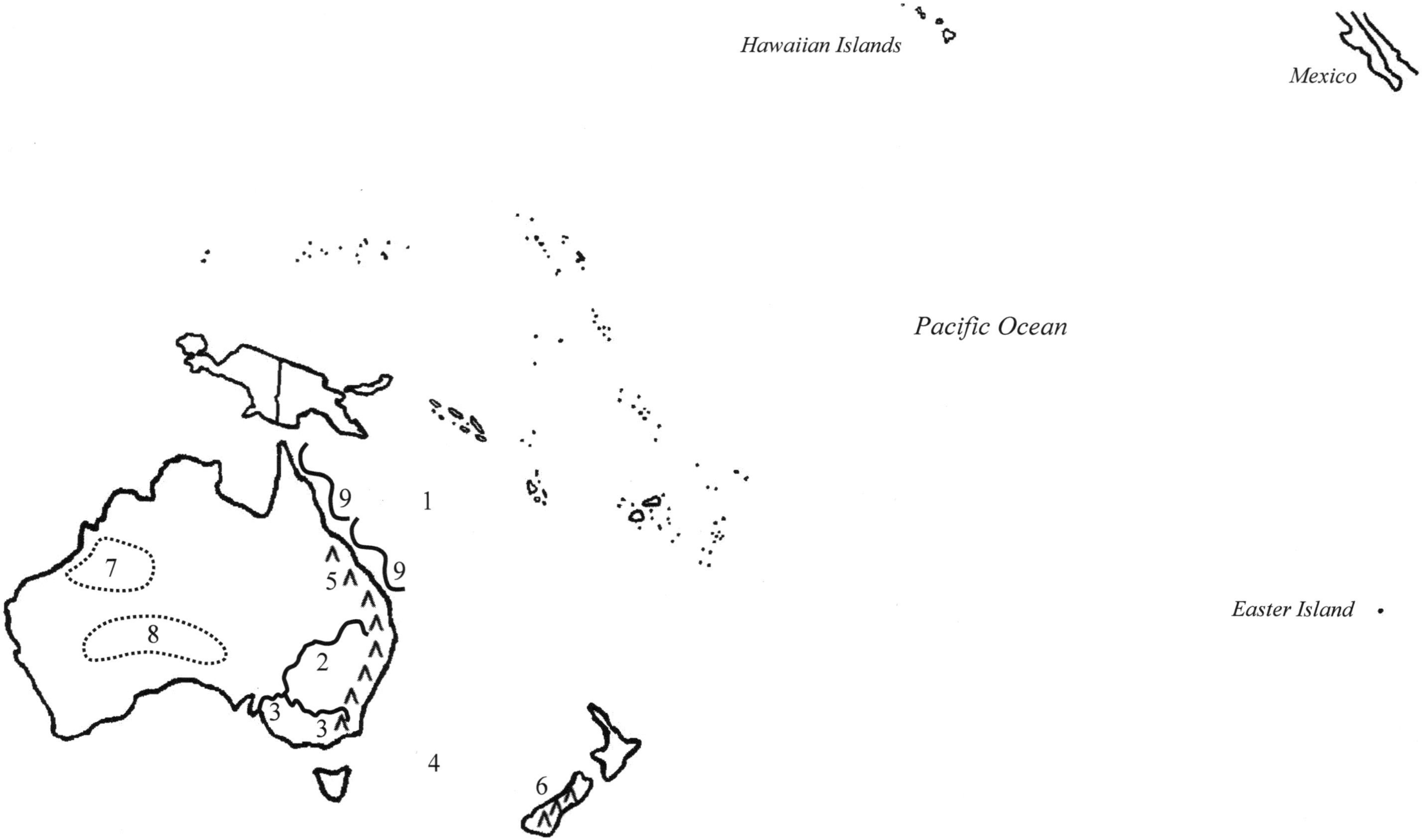

Hawaiian Islands

Mexico

Pacific Ocean

Easter Island •

9

1

7

5

9

8

2

3

3

4

6

OCEANIC BODIES OF WATER, MOUNTAINS, DESERTS, REEF

Match the correct physical feature with its number on the page above.

1. _____   A. Coral

2. _____   B. Darling

3. _____   C. Great Barrier

4. _____   D. Great Dividing Range

5. _____   E. Great Sandy

6. _____   F. Great Victorian

7. _____   G. Murray

8. _____   H. Southern Alps

9. _____   I. Tasman

UNIT 6: SOUTH AMERICAN TESTS

SOUTH AMERICAN COUNTRIES, ISLANDS

Match the correct country with its number on the page above.

1. _____   A. Argentina

2. _____   B. Bolivia

3. _____   C. Brazil

4. _____   D. Chile

5. _____   E. Columbia

6. _____   F. Ecuador

7. _____   G. French Guiana

8. _____   H. Galapagos Islands

9. _____   I. Guyana

10. _____   J. Paraguay

11. _____   K. Peru

12. _____   L. Suriname

13. _____   M. Uruguay

14. _____   N. Venezuela

SOUTH AMERICN CAPITALS

Match the correct capital with its number on the page above.

1. _____   A.   Asuncion

2. _____   B.   Bogota

3. _____   C.   Brasilia

4. _____   D.   Buenos Aires

5. _____   E.   Caracas

6. _____   F.   Cayenne

7. _____   G.   Georgetown

8. _____   H.   La Pas

9. _____   I.   Lima

10. _____   J.   Montevideo

    _____   K.   Paramaribo

11. _____   L.   Quito

12. _____   M.   Santiago

13. _____   N.   Sucre

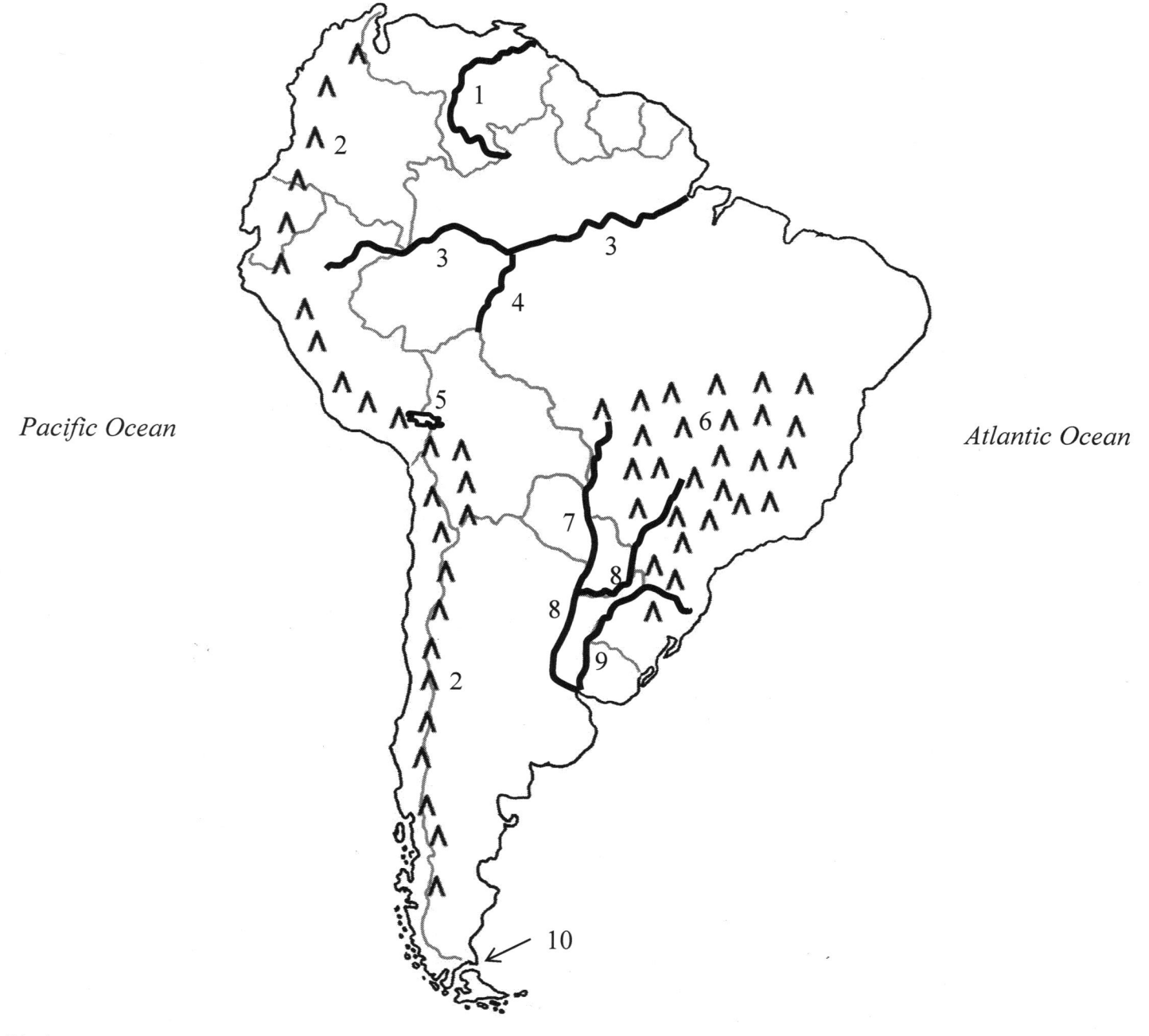

Pacific Ocean

Atlantic Ocean

SOUTH AMERICAN BODIES OF WATER, MOUNTAINS

Match the correct geographical feature with its number on the page above.

1. _____   A. Amazon

2. _____   B. Andes

3. _____   C. Brazilian Highlands

4. _____   D. Titicaca

5. _____   E. Madeira

6. _____   F. Orinoco

7. _____   G. Paraguay

8. _____   H. Paraná

9. _____   I. Magellan

10. _____   J. Uruguay